THE *Neat Stuff*
SOMETHING-TO-DO BOOK

by
Thomas F. Ris

Art Direction and Design by Kathy Eitner
Illustrated by Deborah Bratlein, Dale Nordell,
Marcia Pomeroy, Kelly Smith, John Smith

WANDERER BOOKS NEW YORK

Copyright©1979 by Thomas F. Ris
All rights reserved
including the right of reproduction
in whole or in part in any form
Published by Wanderer Books
A Simon & Schuster Division of
Gulf & Western Corporation
Simon & Schuster Building
1230 Avenue of the Americas
New York, New York 10020

Manufactured in the United States of America

1 2 3 4 5 6 7 8 9 10

Library of Congress Cataloging in Publication Data

Ris, Thomas F
  The neat stuff something-to-do book.

   SUMMARY: Includes jokes, riddles, experiments, games,
exercises, ways to earn money, recipes, and arts and crafts,
and offers suggestions for starting a Neat Stuff Club of your
own.
   1. Amusements—Juvenile literature.   2. Creative
activities and seat work—Juvenile literature.
3. Riddles—Juvenile literature.   4. Handicraft—Juvenile
literature.   [1. Amusements.   2. Handicraft]   I. Bratlein,
Deborah.   II. Title.
GV1203.R53   1979b   031'.02   79-16633

ISBN 0-671-33079-9

Also available in Julian Messner Library Edition

Dedicated to two really neat people
with love ... Kate and John

CONTENTS

Neat Stuff

THIS IS YOUR
SOMETHING-TO-DO BOOK

Inside this book, you'll find super ideas for games, experiments, ways to earn money, special recipes and lots of different ways to celebrate many holidays throughout the year.

With this book, you learn how to start your very own NEAT STUFF Club. You'll always know NEAT STUFF Club members by the special Club whistle and the very secret Club handshake.

You'll also find special directions for making your own Secret Club Code Machine. Then you'll be ready to send and receive private messages from friends. No one will ever know your most secret messages!

If that's not enough, then laugh yourself silly with the crazy and wild jokes and riddles.

It's all here in your SOMETHING-TO-DO BOOK.

START YOUR OWN CLUB

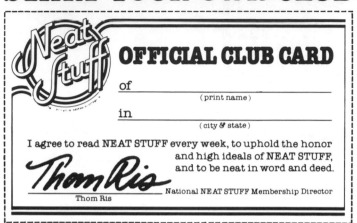

OFFICIAL CLUB CARD

of _____
                (print name)

in _____
                (city & state)

I agree to read NEAT STUFF every week, to uphold the honor
and high ideals of NEAT STUFF,
and to be neat in word and deed.

Thom Ris _____ National NEAT STUFF Membership Director

Thom Ris

Join with kids from all over the country who already have their own NEAT STUFF Clubs.

A NEAT STUFF Club is simple to start. Just get together with a group of friends and elect a president, vice-president, secretary, treasurer and a jester (usually the funniest kid in your neighborhood). It's fun to have elections about every two weeks, then everyone gets to be a club officer.

Hold regular club meetings to work on the NEAT STUFF projects that you will find in this book.

If you want, you can have club dues. A few cents, a nickel or dime each week or month will help you buy some of the things you'll want for your super projects and activities.

You can even make your own NEAT STUFF Club Membership Cards for everyone. Trace or photocopy this card. Then fill in your name plus the name of your city and state.

Carry your NEAT STUFF Club membership Card always. It's the neat thing to do!

NEAT STUFF CLUB HANDSHAKE

Now you can find out who is a member of a NEAT STUFF Club very quickly. When you meet a friend, or someone you think might be a NEAT STUFF Club Member, give him or her the official handshake.

Here's how:
Grasp your friend around the wrist and give two quick shakes. If he or she returns the handshake with three quick shakes, then you've got a real friend.

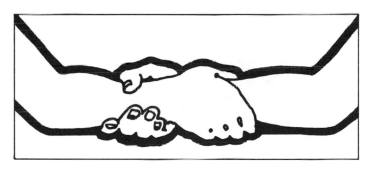

...AND WHISTLE

If you cannot shake someone's hand, but still want to know if he or she is a NEAT STUFF person, try the NEAT STUFF Whistle. It's simple. Just whistle the musical notes (da, dit, dit, da) twice. If he or she responds with the same notes three times, you're really in luck!

OFFICIAL SECRET CODE MACHINE

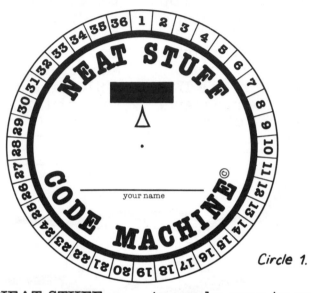

Circle 1.

For all NEAT STUFF Club Members, here's a super way to receive and send top-secret messages using your very own Official Code Machine. It has four different code combinations so that you can fool even the nosiest person.

To make your own, trace on a piece of paper or photocopy the two circles on this page. If you trace, be sure to carefully follow all the marks! Then cut out your copy of these two circles and glue them to heavy cardboard. Punch a hole in the center of both circles. Cut out the small black area inside circle number one. Then connect the circles with a clip, so that both circles turn easily.

A PAPER FASTENER LIKE THIS WORKS BEST

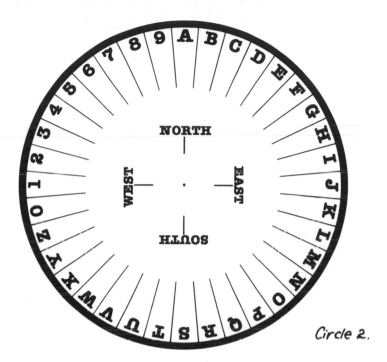

Circle 2.

Here's how it works:
1. Turn the top circle to one of the four compass directions: North, East, South or West.
2. Hold the circles tightly. The numbers on the smaller circle will point to letters or numbers on the larger circle. The numbers on the smaller circle are the code. The letters and numbers on the big circle are the message.

Here's an example:
South Code
7 33 3 : 19 36 23 : 19 :
1 3 34 23 36 :
34 23 36 1 9 32.
You are a super person.

East Code
30 28 5 : 16 6 12 :
14 36 5 2 :
14 35 32 5 : 16 6 12 :
14 35 36 10 11 3 32.
Can you wink when you whistle?

KEEP NEAT STUFF CLUB RECORDS

NEAT STUFF CLUB MINUTES

Place of Meeting: Date of Meeting:

President: Treasurer:

Vice-President: Jester:

Secretary:

What we did at this meeting:

_____

_____

_____

_____

Dues collected at the meeting: $_____

It's fun to keep a record, or "minutes," of each NEAT STUFF Club meeting. In this way, you can easily remember the officers, the amount of dues members paid, and all of your projects.

Here's a simple form you can use for your NEAT STUFF Club minutes.

JOKES AND RIDDLES

Hans: How many women are born in Germany?
Fritz: None! Only babies are born in Germany.

Esky: Why are polar bears inexpensive pets to keep?
Mo: Because they live on ice.

Pit: What did one wall say to the other wall?
Pat: I'll meet you at the corner.

Q: If a Czar's wife is called a Czarina, what do you call her children?
A: Czardines.

Ed: Why did the man go over the hill?
Fred: Because he couldn't walk through it!

Mom: What is a baby after it's six months old?
Dad: Seven months old.

Customer: Can this sweater be worn in the rain?
Clerk: Have you ever seen sheep carry umbrellas?

Customer: May I try on those pants in the window?
Clerk: I'd suggest you use the dressing room instead.

Customer: Are you serving crabs today?
Waiter: Sure, we'll serve anyone who wants to eat here.

Q: What do mother giraffes have that no other animal has?
A: Baby giraffes.

JOKES AND RIDDLES

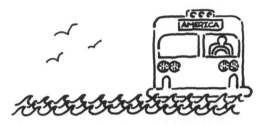

Billy: Which bus crossed the ocean in 1492?
Silly: I don't know.
Billy: The Columbus.

Jack: If you don't know a rope trick, what can you do?
Jill: Skip it!

Silly: What has a lot of teeth but no mouth?
Sally: I don't know.
Silly: A comb.

Will: If two is company and three is a crowd, what is four and five?
Bill: Nine!

Q: Why can't you tell secrets in a cornfield?
A: Because the corn has ears.

Mom: What is clean on the outside and grey on the inside?
Dad: What is?
Mom: An elephant in a Baggie.

Mick: What is white and floats through the air and lands on all the trees and ground?
Mike: Snow flakes.

Q: What do you call a feeble mountain?
A: A weak peak

Knock Knock
Who's there?
King Kong
King Kong who?
King Kong the wicked witch is dead.

EXPERIMENTS

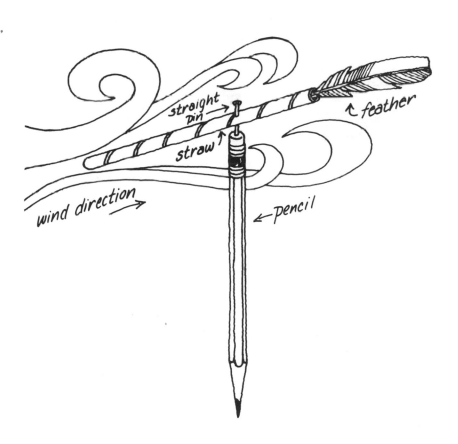

straight pin →

↑ feather

straw ↑

← pencil

wind direction →

HAIRY POTATO HEAD

A fun activity is growing a grassy green head of "hair" on a potato. It's really easy. Here's how.

You'll need: A big potato, knife and spoon, cotton, grass seed, a plate or bowl, two buttons, straight pins and cloves.

Cut off the top of the potato and throw it away. Scoop out the inside of the rest of the potato so that there is a hole about an inch or so deep. Stuff the cotton into the hole. Sprinkle water on the cotton so that it is very wet. Then put grass seed on top of the wet cotton. Keep your potato head in a bowl or on a plate.

Wow, in a few days you'll have a potato with a green head of "hair"! Use the pins to attach the buttons on the potato for eyes. The cloves will make a happy or sad mouth.

For fun, give your potato head a haircut!

WEATHER VANE

It's fun know which way the wind is blowing. A weather vane is the instrument people use to tell the direction of the wind. Here's how you can make a super weather vane.

You'll need:
- One drinking straw
- One straight pin
- One feather
- One pencil with an eraser

Directions:

First, put the feather into one end of the straw. Then find the balancing point or exact center of the straw. Put the pin through the straw at the balancing point. Then push the pin into the pencil eraser. There should be a small space between the straw and the pencil. Put the pencil into the ground, and your weather vane is ready to tell you the direction in which the wind is blowing. The weather vane will point into the direction of the wind.

RAIN GAUGE

Suggested by
Tom Valentine

Tom Valentine of Assumption School in Seattle has a great way to make a rain gauge which really works. It's simple to make. You'll need: a jar, a ruler, a grease pencil or waterproof pen, paper tape, a measuring cup, water and some motor oil.

Here are Tom's directions:

"Mark off the ruler in centimeters (one inch equals 2.54 centimeters) with a grease pencil or pen. Fix the ruler inside the jar with the paper tape. Pour 10 centimeters of water into the jar. Then carefully add a small amount of motor oil on top of the water to prevent evaporation."

"Place the rain gauge jar outdoors in an open spot. It's a good idea to put bricks around the jar to prevent the wind or pets from knocking it over."

"Measure the amount of rain collected on top of the oil each day. Keep a weekly record of the rainfall in your town."

SEE THE VEINS IN PLANTS

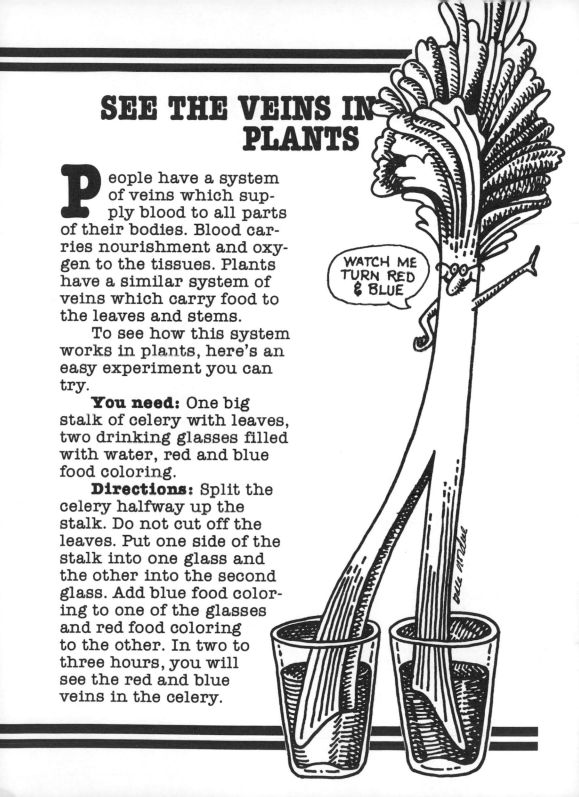

People have a system of veins which supply blood to all parts of their bodies. Blood carries nourishment and oxygen to the tissues. Plants have a similar system of veins which carry food to the leaves and stems.

To see how this system works in plants, here's an easy experiment you can try.

You need: One big stalk of celery with leaves, two drinking glasses filled with water, red and blue food coloring.

Directions: Split the celery halfway up the stalk. Do not cut off the leaves. Put one side of the stalk into one glass and the other into the second glass. Add blue food coloring to one of the glasses and red food coloring to the other. In two to three hours, you will see the red and blue veins in the celery.

COMMUNICATE WITH YOUR FRIENDS

Make your own walkie-talkie so that you can talk privately with a friend. All you need are two clean cans, string, hammer, nails and a candle.

Punch holes in the center of each can with the nail. Thread the string through the holes, and knot the ends inside the cans. The string can be any length. It must be long enough to reach your friend, but short enough so that it does not touch the ground. Keep the string tight. If it touches anything, the sound of your voice will not carry. To improve the sound, wax the string by rubbing it with a candle.

COMMUNICATE WITH THE WORLD

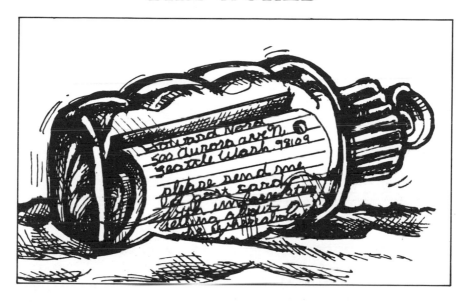

To find out where the water in local streams or rivers travels or the direction of the ocean tides, try this easy communications experiment.

Get a clear plastic bottle with a tight lid. Then write a message and put it into the bottle. Your message should include your name, age, address and maybe your hobbies. Be sure to ask whoever finds your bottle and message to send you a postcard or letter telling where your bottle was discovered.

When your message is prepared and tightly sealed in the bottle, throw it into a local stream or moving water. It might completely disappear or it could float just a few miles or around the world!

PLAN A FIRE ESCAPE ROUTE

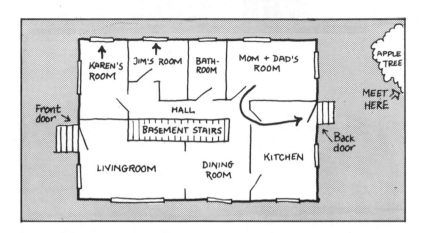

It's always important to think about fire safety at home and school. In addition to being on the lookout for fire hazards around the house, it's also a good idea to plan fire escape routes should there be a fire.

It's simple to do. Draw a floor plan of your entire house, including the upstairs if you live in a two-story house. Be sure to draw in every window and door. Then, sit down with all the members of your family to decide the route each will take in case there is a fire. Plan on more than one escape route from various rooms since fire could be burning in a number of places in the house.

At the same time, decide with your family upon a meeting place outside the house. If there is a fire, everyone should go to the meeting place and wait for other members of the family. Then you'll know if everyone is safe.

It's neat to think and be safe!

MEASURE AIR POLLUTION

Air pollution cannot always be seen, since it is often invisible to the eye. You can find out if you have air pollution in your neighborhood with this experiment. All you need is a clean glass jar with a lid and some clean white paper.

To see if you have continuing air pollution, repeat this experiment every week, or whenever it rains or snows. Keep a record. In a notebook or on a sheet of paper, write the date, weather conditions, such as cloudy, sunny, snow, etc., and whether or not you have air pollution. Just for fun, try this experiment at different times of the year. Find out if there is more or less air pollution in the summer, in the winter or in other seasons.

On a snowy or rainy day, put the jar outside on a window sill or someplace in the yard where pets will not disturb it. After you've collected snow or rain water, bring the jar inside and cover it with a lid.

1. When the snow has melted, hold the jar up to a strong light to see if there are any tiny specks floating in the water. If there are, you have air pollution.

2. Put some of the water on a piece of white paper. Does the water make the paper turn colors? If so, you have air pollution.

3. Let the water sit in the jar for several days. If dirt or grey film appears at the bottom of the jar, then you have air pollution.

CHEMISTRY EXPERIMENT

A word often used in the world of chemistry is precipitation. Precipitation, pronounced pree-sip-i-ta-shun, refers to a thing which falls down. For example, if the weather bureau predicts precipitation, some type of moisture will probably fall from the clouds.

Here is an experiment you can do at home to see precipitation.

You'll need: Epsom salts; clear, unscented household ammonia; water; a clear drinking glass; and a tablespoon. (Ammonia is poison, so be careful using it—recap the bottle tightly right after use—especially when little children are around.)

Put three tablespoons of Epsom salts into one-fourth glass of water. Stir until all Epsom salts are dissolved. Fill the glass with ammonia. Stir again. You will see a precipitation of white magnesium hydroxide (milk of magnesia) falling in the water.

When you finish with this experiment, pour all the water and ammonia down the drain just to be safe. Carefully wash the glass and spoon with lots of soap and water. Then rinse them both at least twice. This will prevent poisoning anyone who uses them later on.

BLOWING BUBBLES

You can make a brew which is great for blowing bubbles. It's very simple. Get a cup of water, liquid detergent, cooking oil and some stove-pipe wire.

Add a dash of detergent and a small amount of cooking oil to the cup of water. Then bend the wire so that it looks the same as a circle with a tail.

Dip the wire into the soapy brew and ... blow ... great bubbles.

MAKE A TIME MACHINE

Build a time machine, then you will know how much time you spend talking on the telephone, taking a bath or running a race.

You need: Two short glass bottles with lids, glue that sticks to metal, either salt or sand, a hammer and a strong nail.

Wash and dry the bottles and caps. While the caps are off the bottles, glue them together. When the glue is dry, use the hammer and nail to punch a big hole in the caps. Careful of your fingers! Fill one of the bottles with either salt or sand. Screw the lids to each of the bottles. Turn the time machine over, and watch the sand or salt run into the empty bottle.

Using a clock or watch with a second hand, time how long it takes for the salt or sand to run from one bottle to another. Remove or add sand or salt until your time machine measures one, two or three minutes.

JOKES AND RIDDLES

WHAT DO YOU CALL THE FIRE CHIEF'S DAUGHTER?

MISCHIEF!

Tom: What has four legs and only one foot?
Tim: A bed.

Customer: Do you have any wild duck?
Waiter: No, but I can take a tame duck and make it mad!

Fred: Did you ever tickle a mule?
Red: No, why?
Fred: Because you'd get a big kick out of it!

She: Why did the boy take hay to bed?
He: To feed his nightmare.

Lee: Who likes to have people for dinner?
Roy: A cannibal.

Poison: What did the termite say to the tree?
Ivy: It's been nice gnawing you!

First Aid Teacher: What would you do if your sister swallowed a pencil?
First Aid Student: Use a pen.

Q: What happens when cooks get mad?
A: They beat the eggs and whip the cream.

JOKES AND RIDDLES

Ray: What is a greasy flyer?
Better: I don't know.
Ray: A dirty bird.

Wall: What tree is like a pet?
Nut: A Pussywillow.

Cotton: Who can jump as high as a tree?
Wood: Anyone. Trees can't jump.

John: Why did the soldier salute his TV?
Greg: Why?
John: Because it was General Electric.

Farmer: What has a pen but can't write?
Banker: I don't know
Farmer: A pig!

Knock Knock
Who's there?
Chester!
Chester who?
Chester minute and I'll tell you.

Kate: Why is a mousetrap like the chicken pox?
John: Because it's always catching.

Knock Knock
Who's there?
Ima
Ima who?
Ima tired of your knock knock jokes.

Mit: Why is a president like a carpenter?
Mat: Why?
Mit: Because both can make cabinets.

Knock Knock
Who's there?
Cargo
Cargo who?
Cargo beep beep.

GAMES AND EXERCISES

TASMANIAN HOPSCOTCH GAME

Tasmanian Hopscotch is a form of the favorite old game of hopscotch—only more difficult!

Draw a large snail, such as the one on this page, in an open area or on a concrete floor using chalk. Start your drawing from the center; it's easier. Divide the snail into spaces, as pictured. Make as many spaces as possible, but be sure that each one is big enough to stand or hop in. Starting from the middle of the snail, write the word REST in every fourth space. Have at least five REST spots.

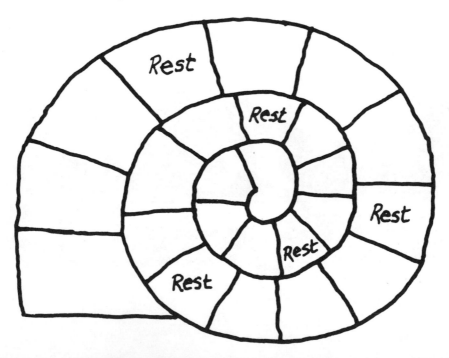

To play, one person at a time hops from one space to another on just ONE foot, the same foot. Both feet are allowed on the spaces marked REST.

When the end of the snail is reached, hop back on the other foot. If some-one changes feet or steps on a line, the player has to start over again from the beginning.

After a player jumps all the way in and out of the snail, write that per-son's name on any space. That space is a rest spot

ONLY for that person. Other players must hop completely over that space.

The winner is the per-son whose name is in the most spaces.

INVENTING STORIES FOR LAUGHS

Get together with a group of your friends or members of your NEAT STUFF Club. Ask everyone to bring a favorite book.

Form a circle. Then sit, lie or fall down! One person begins to read, starting anyplace in his or her book—back, middle or front.

Everyone takes a turn reading just one paragraph. Going around the circle, continue taking turns reading. The story will sound so silly that you begin to laugh, and before you know it, everyone will join in.

Keep reading until you can't stop laughing. Then start all over again.

JAPANESE TIC-TAC-TOE

Here is a good game
for two NEAT STUFF
Club members to play
at home, in the car, or
during recess at school.

Get a large sheet of
paper and draw horizontal
and vertical lines over the
whole page. The first
player makes a circle

around any intersection of
four squares, as shown.
Then the second player
adds an X at the corners of
another four squares. The
player who wins the game
will have five X's or circles
running in a straight line
in any direction.

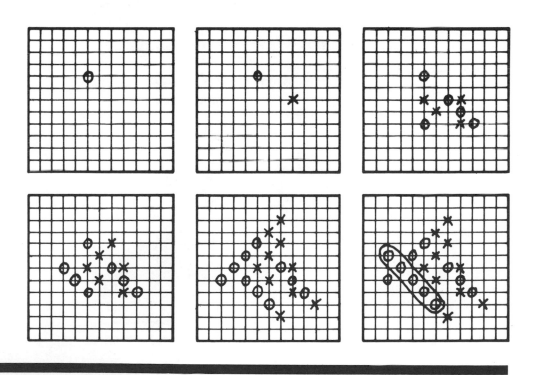

LIMBO FOR EXERCISE
AND LAUGHS

This is the name of a dance which started in the Caribbean. It is also a great game if you want to stretch a little, get some exercise and lots of laughs.

Get together three or more friends or NEAT STUFF Club members and a long pole. Two people should hold the pole two or three feet off the ground. Taking turns, each person bends backwards and wiggles his or her way under the pole without touching it.

Players cannot bend forward or sideways, only backwards! A player who touches the pole or falls over is out of that game. Keep lowering the pole, after everyone has had a turn, until it is too low for anyone to get under. The last player who can get under the pole without touching it or the ground is the winner.

Musical limbo is lots of fun too, only faster! Turn on the radio or play a very fast record. Players should try to keep time with the music as they struggle to get under the pole.

WINTER EXERCISES

During the winter, it's not always easy to get enough exercise. Yet exercise is important to everyone's health. It helps the heart and lungs, and prevents stiff joints while building muscles.

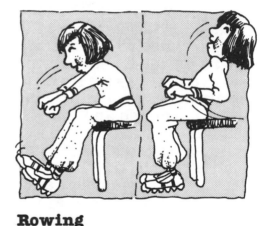

Jogging on the Spot
Keeping your toes on the floor, raise your heels, first the left, then the right, as high as possible. At the same time, raise your arms in a bent position. Rock backward and forward. Continue for one to three minutes.

Rowing
Stretch your arms in front of you while bending the upper part of your body forward for a rowing "stroke." With your heels on the floor, lift up the forward part of your feet, then press your toes down. Draw in your arms, and at the same time move your body backwards, completing the "stroke." Repeat for one to three minutes.

Here are some exercises you can do while sitting in a chair. They are sugggested by Scandinavian Airlines for airplane passengers. The first two are warm-up exercises; the next two are good for blood circulation.

Knee Raising
Grasp your left leg with both hands and pull it up. Do the same with the right one, then both legs. Repeat this exercise ten times for each leg and both together.

Slalom-Skiing
Sit with your legs as far out to the right as possible, and both arms on the right side. Lift your heels up and swing your legs all the way over to the left, while swinging your arms over in the same direction. Repeat this exercise thirty times.

JOKES AND RIDDLES

Jay: This sandwich is bad.
Mike: Who told you?
Jay: A little swallow!

Kate: I saw a man-eating shark at the aquarium.
John: So what! I saw a woman eating a salmon in a restaurant.

First Lady Cannibal: I don't know what to make of my husband these days.
Second Lady Cannibal: Let me give you a new recipe I think you'll like.

Gail: Where did the pilgrims stand when they landed on Plymouth Rock?
Sam: I don't know.
Gail: On their feet!

Phil: How do you keep a turkey in suspense?
Bill: How?
Phil: I'll tell you tomorrow.

Pat: How long can a turkey stand on one leg?
Mike: I don't know, how long?
Pat: Try it and see.

Jay: What happens when a monster chases a banana?
Mike: What happens?
Jay: The banana splits.

Bo: There's lots of juice in this grapefruit.
Peep: I'll say, more than meets the eye.

Q: What letter of the alphabet can you drink?
A: Tea!

MAKING DOLLARS AND CENTS

MAKE AND SELL NEWSPAPER LOGS

You can make logs for burning in a fireplace out of newspapers. And they will burn almost as well as wood.

You'll need:
- Lots of old papers
- A big tub or pan
- A long stick or broom handle
- Liquid detergent

Follow instructions one through four on the opposite page.

To make sure the logs are dry, test them in the fireplace to see how well and how long they will burn. You might make the logs thicker or thinner, depending on how well they burn.

When you have several dozen dry logs, you are ready to sell them. Charge 25¢ each or maybe 5 for $1.00. This is a good way to make some cool cash with a hot item!

1. Fill a tub with water and add a couple of squirts of detergent.

2. Soak a one-inch stack of folded newspapers in the tub.

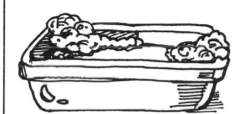

3. Roll the wet papers tightly around the stick, and squeeze out the water. Add another layer around the first, squeezing as you go.

4. When the log is two or three inches thick, remove the stick and put the rolls in a warm place to dry.

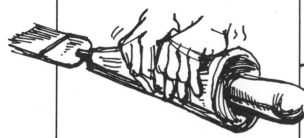

DOG-WALKING SERVICE

A good way to earn extra money and have fun at the same time is to work for neighbors and friends. Start a dog-walking service.

First, make some cards to advertise your service. Be sure to include the times when you are available, the cost of the service (usually about 50¢ per hour), your name, address and telephone number. Distribute the cards to people in your neighborhood who have dogs.

As a little treat, you might carry a couple of dog biscuits in your pocket to give to the dog at the end of the walk. This is a good way to satisfy your customers.

Now, for some important tips about this business:

1. Use a short leash so that you will have better control of the dog.
2. Never walk big dogs which you cannot control.
3. Never leave the dog alone.
4. Take your time. Dogs like to poke along.
5. Respect neighbors' yards. Do not let dog use sidewalks or lawns for a bathroom. In fact, in New York City you'll be fined for not picking up your dog's droppings. Learn the laws of your community.

SNOW-SHOVELING SERVICE

hen winter comes and snow is on the way, you and members of your NEAT STUFF Club can set up a Snow-Shoveling Service. It's a good idea to get organized before the first snowflakes fall so that you'll be ready for action. Remember, everyone must be willing to work hard shoveling snow, no matter how cold it gets.

One of the first things to do is prepare advertisements and distribute them to neighbors in your area.

Your announcement should list the telephone number of one person, who will be responsible for dispatching others to shovel walks and driveways, plus the hours all of you are available to work.

Be sure everyone has a good snowshovel. Then distribute your advertisements. You'll be in Snow Biz!

MAKING POPCORN GARLANDS

Some people like the old-fashioned look of popcorn garlands on Christmas trees. However, for one reason or another, they may not want to make them. So you can have some extra money for Christmas gifts by making popcorn garlands to sell. But don't wait until the last minute. Have them ready in plenty of time for decorating.

To start, make lots of popcorn. Do not add salt or butter. Get strong, white thread and a needle. Thread the needle and begin stringing the popcorn on two-to-three-foot lengths of thread.

When you sell the popcorn garlands, remind your customers to put them on their outside trees after Christmas. This will give the birds a nice New Year's snack.

BUILD BIRD FEEDERS

In the winter, many birds fly south. However, some birds stay in colder areas. They can always use some extra food, and you can help them, plus make some money too!

Build bird feeders to sell to friends and neighbors. Your customers help the birds and so do you.

Here's how:

1. Cut out one side of a half-gallon milk carton as shown.
2. Cut a hole in the top and put a heavy string through it.
3. Paint the outside with enamel.
4. Put a small stick or dowel through both sides of the bottom for a perch.
5. Hang it from a tree or set on a windowsill.

After you have finished making your bird feeders, buy a big bag of wild birdseed and fill the bottom of each bird feeder.

When you sell a feeder, be sure to remind your customer to put it where cats or squirrels cannot harm the birds or eat their food.

SAVINGS ACCOUNTS

Now that you're earning money, or have received some as a gift, what do you plan to do with it? If you want to save it for a vacation, a new bike, or some super clothes, it's a good idea to put the money into a savings account. It will be safer there (since you won't be tempted to use it when you are broke), and it will also "earn interest."

When money earns interest, a bank pays you for letting them keep your money. The amount of interest your money earns depends on how much you deposit in your account and how long you leave it there.

To open a savings account, get your Mom or Dad, or some adult over 18 years old, to go with you to a bank. If you are under 18 years old, it is usually necessary to open a "joint account" with a parent or

guardian. This means that you and one of your parents or your guardian sign the application which starts your savings account.

Both of you will have to sign a withdrawal slip if you want to take money out of your savings account. However, you can deposit money by yourself whenever you like!

GET A SOCIAL SECURITY CARD

Everyone in the United States who works, and even people who do not work regularly have a social security card. When you work for a company, a small part of your salary is paid to the Social Security Administration. If you do odd jobs, such as shoveling snow, you do not have to pay social security. At age sixty-two, or if you are disabled, you can apply to start receiving the money which you have paid to the Social Security Administration. The amount you receive each month depends on how much money you have earned.

Anyone can get a social security card. It costs nothing. The government keeps track of the money you pay to the Social Security Administration. Each card has a number which is your number for life!

You can apply for a social security card by calling the Social Security Administration (listed in the telephone directory under U.S. Government in most cities). Anyone under 18 can send for an application for a card by mail. You can also visit your local Social Security Administration office. It will take about two months to receive your own Social Security Card.

JOKES AND RIDDLES

Rob: What did the curtain say to the window?
Roy: What?
Rob: Don't move, I've got you covered.

Q: If an egg floats down the middle of the Mississippi River, where does it come from?
A: From a chicken.

Knock Knock
Who's there?
Howard
Howard who?
Howard you like a kiss?

Tee: What kind of fish do you find in a birdcage?
Hee: I don't know
Tee: A perch!

Silly: That dog must have swallowed a clock.
Sally: How do you know?
Silly: He's full of ticks.

First Race Horse: Do you remember me?
Second Race Horse: Your pace is familiar, but I don't remember the mane.

Bill: What did the teacher say when she lost her glass eyeball?
Phyl: What did she say?
Bill: There goes my favorite pupil.

Tom: I'm taking French, Russian and Algebra in school this year.
Jerry: Oh really. Let me hear you say "good night" in Algebra.

Knock Knock
Who's there?
Duane
Duane who?
Duane the bathtub, I'm drowning!

HOLIDAYS

GUNG HAY FAHT CHOY

Means Happy New Year in Chinese

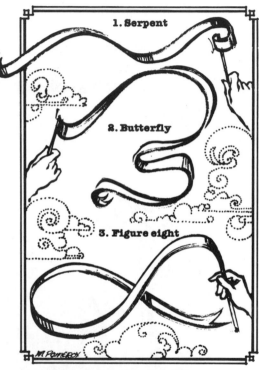

1. Serpent

2. Butterfly

3. Figure eight

M. POMEROY

During the Chinese New Year, which usually starts sometime during mid-February and lasts for over a week, it is the custom to have colorful celebrations and parades.

Chinese youngsters add to the fun with ribbon dances which are very colorful. To prepare for a ribbon dance, get a piece of crepe paper or ribbon. It should be over 2 inches wide and over 18 inches long. Tape the ribbon or crepe paper to a pencil or an old chopstick! Then, holding it in your hand, do some dance step and wave your arms. You can easily make all the different designs shown on this page.

Happy New Year, Chinese style!

"Gung Hay Faht Choy" calligraphy by Willard Jue.

WHO IS ST. PATRICK?

Born in the Fifth century in Britain, St. Patrick is a popular folk hero of the Irish. Legends tell that he was responsible for driving the snakes out of Ireland. Many say that St. Patrick was the first person to write Irish poetry and use the shamrock for the Irish national symbol.

On St. Patrick's Day, greet your Irish friends by saying, **"Erin Go Bragh"** (pronounced, air in go bra) which is an ancient battle cry meaning **Ireland Forever**!

Don't Get Pinched!

The Irish often pinch people who don't wear green on St. Patrick's Day. To protect yourself from pinchers, trace this shamrock onto a piece of paper, color it green, cut it out and wear it on St. Patrick's Day. Wear green on March 17, the day of this Irish celebration.

ERIN GO BRAGH

DECORATE EASTER EGGS

Here are three different ways you can decorate eggs for Easter.

1. Hard boil and cool the eggs first. Then, coat them with Elmer's Glue. Let the glue dry slightly. The eggs will be sticky, so keep them on waxed paper so they won't stick to the table. (It's a good idea to wash your hands after coating each egg.) Roll each egg in dry, uncooked rice. For color, glue small dried flowers to the egg.

2. Hardboil and cool the eggs. Dip small, shell-shaped macaroni into commercial Easter egg dye until they are colored. Then glue the macaroni all over the eggs.

3. To make an Easter egg look as though it is made of real marble, wrap an uncooked egg in the brown skin of an onion. Carefully tie the onion skin around the egg with a string. Then tie a small piece of cloth tightly around the onion skin. Boil the egg for 30 minutes. Unwrap it and it will look like real marble!

EGGSHELL PLANTERS

Here's a great way to reuse your Easter egg shells after the eggs are eaten. Plant flower and vegetable seeds in them. When you crack the eggs, try to get at least one-half of the shell to remain in one piece. It's not always easy to do. However, if you hit the egg with a dull knife at the place where you want it to crack, chances for success will be pretty good. Once you've cracked it and removed the contents, carefully wash and dry the shells. With a pin, gently poke a small hole in the bottom of the egg for drainage.

Place the half-shells into a regular egg carton. Fill them with a mixture of sand and clean dirt. Get seeds from a local store and plant them in the shells. Be sure to follow the directions on the seed package. As the seeds start to grow, remove, or "thin out," the smaller or weaker shoots.

When your young plants are healthy, and the weather is warm enough for them to be outside, transplant them to your garden. To protect the young plants, it is wise to cover them at night.

HALLOWEEN MONSTER ROBOT

For Halloween fun, make a monster robot that looks as if it's from outer space.

Here are some of the things you can use: egg cartons, matchboxes, cardboard tubes, string or yarn, plastic or paper cups, construction paper, small packing boxes, wire, springs, balls, or ping-pong balls, paper plates, and milk cartons.

Once you have a lot of different materials, lay them out and decide which should be used for the head, body, legs, and arms.

Fasten the materials together with tape, wire, glue, or staples. Paint the monster if you wish. Yarn or string are good for making hair. Balls can be used for the eyes.

Monster Robots are a great way to scare all your friends on Halloween, or any other time.

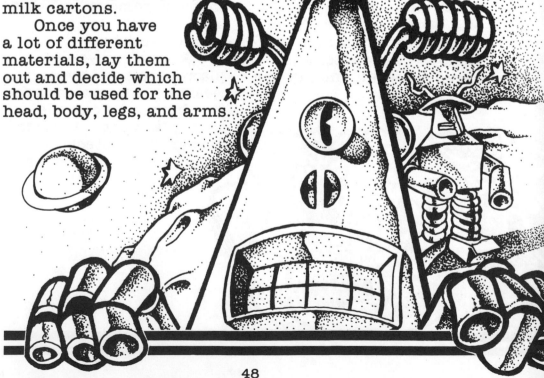

THANKSGIVING DECORATIONS

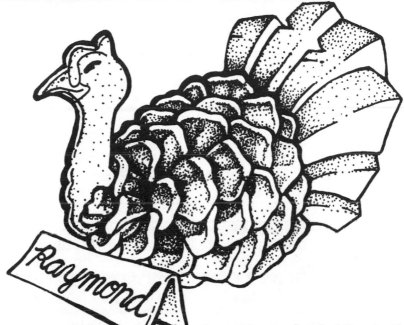

You can make great decorations or placecards for your Thanksgiving table.

Get some pinecones. A park is a good place to look for them. Or on your own property or a neighbor's. But get permission first. Cut turkey heads from colored construction paper. Glue the head to one end of the pinecones.

Get more colored paper and cut it into various lengths to look like tail feathers. Stick the feathers into the pinecone and glue them in place.

Arrange the pinecone turkeys as a centerpiece for the table, or place one at each setting with a card, or do both. To make the placecards, print the name of each guest on a small piece of paper and place it in front or on top of the turkey.

GLITTER CHRISTMAS CARDS

Glitter cards are a sparkling way of saying Merry Christmas.

Buy some glitter in any color you like, at a hobby or stationery store. Also get some colored paper, such as 3 × 5 unlined index cards, and envelopes to fit.

Light-colored glitter looks great on dark paper and vice versa! Some good greetings are, "Have a Cool Yule," "Noel," or "Peace."

When your glitter cards are completed, you're ready to address the envelopes and mail them.

1. CUT COLORED PAPER TO FIT IN YOUR ENVELOPES

2. PAINT YOUR DESIGN WITH A SMALL BRUSH DIPPED IN GLUE

3. BEFORE THE GLUE DRIES, SPRINKLE ON THE GLITTER

4. WAIT A FEW MINUTES, THEN SHAKE OFF EXTRA

HERB VINEGAR CHRISTMAS PRESENT

If you are giving a Christmas present to someone who likes to cook, here is a nifty idea for a gift you can make!

You'll need:
- A clear, clean bottle with a tight lid or cork
- Cider or wine vinegar
- 3 or 4 tarragon or mint leaves
- One sprig of dill weed
- 2 or 3 cloves of garlic

Place one of the above herbs or garlic cloves into the bottle. Fill the bottle with the vinegar, and seal it tightly. Make a label describing the contents and glue it to the bottle. Let the bottle sit for a month before giving it to your favorite cook.

Try making three or four different kinds of herb vinegar. Tie a ribbon around the neck of each bottle, and you're ready for Christmas giving.

HOW SAFE IS YOUR HOUSE AT CHRISTMAS?

At Christmas time, people like to decorate their schools and and homes. It's fun to make decorations and put them everywhere. But because of all the excitement of the season, some people forget to think about safety.

You can prevent accidents and fires if you look around your home and school, and then answer the questions on this Holiday Safety Test.

If you find something to be unsafe, discuss it with your parents or teacher, and then look again to see if it has been corrected.

What's Your Holiday Safety Score?

If you didn't answer all of the questions in the Holiday Safety Test correctly, make the necessary changes in your holiday decorations in order to have a safe and happy Christmas.

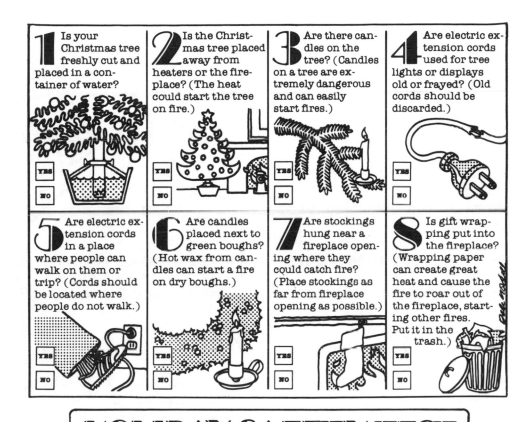

1 Is your Christmas tree freshly cut and placed in a container of water?

YES
NO

2 Is the Christmas tree placed away from heaters or the fireplace? (The heat could start the tree on fire.)

YES
NO

3 Are there candles on the tree? (Candles on a tree are extremely dangerous and can easily start fires.)

YES
NO

4 Are electric extension cords used for tree lights or displays old or frayed? (Old cords should be discarded.)

YES
NO

5 Are electric extension cords in a place where people can walk on them or trip? (Cords should be located where people do not walk.)

YES
NO

6 Are candles placed next to green boughs? (Hot wax from candles can start a fire on dry boughs.)

YES
NO

7 Are stockings hung near a fireplace opening where they could catch fire? (Place stockings as far from fireplace opening as possible.)

YES
NO

8 Is gift wrapping put into the fireplace? (Wrapping paper can create great heat and cause the fire to roar out of the fireplace, starting other fires. Put it in the trash.)

YES
NO

HOLIDAY SAFETY TEST

FOR A NEAT & SAFE CHRISTMAS

ANSWERS: 1 & 2: Yes; 3–8: No

JOKES AND RIDDLES

Tom: What is another word for a dentist's office?
Wendy: I don't know.
Tom: A filling station.

Pam: What do you get when you put salt on a duck's tail?
Bam: I don't know. What do you get?
Pam: Salted quackers, of course.

Q: What has hands but no fingers?
A: A clock.

Rob: Did anyone laugh when the fat man fell on the ice?
Roy: No, but the ice made some awful cracks.

Q: How do you catch a squirrel?
A: Climb a tree and act like a nut.

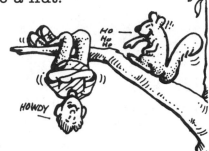

Wally: What do you get when you cross a cocker spaniel, a poodle and a chicken?
Solly: Tell me.
Wally: A cockapoodle do.

Pen: What time is it when an elephant sits on a fence?
Rod: What time?
Pen: Time to get a new fence.

He: What has eyes, but never sees?
She: I don't know.
He: A potato

Neat Stuff

COOKING

JEFF the CHEF

J.C. SMITH

GREAT GOOEY GOOBER BUTTER

THERE'S NUTT'N BUTTER THAN THIS STUFF!

Great news, you can make your own super-tasting goober butter. (Goober is another word for peanut.) It's crunchy, good on sandwiches, and wild when spread on celery.

You'll need:
- One cup of roasted (but not salted) peanuts
- 1 1/2 tablespoons of corn oil
- Salt
- An electric blender or food grinder
- A clean jar with a lid

Remove the peanuts from the shells. Also remove the brown skins from the nuts. If you're using a blender, pour in 1½ tablespoons of corn oil. Set it at top speed, and gradually add the peanuts. Add salt to taste.

When using a food grinder, grind the peanuts two or three times to be sure the mixture is smooth. Add the corn oil, salt lightly and mix with a spoon. Store your goober butter in a clean jar in the refrigerator. You'll go nuts when you taste it.

PICCOLO PIZZA

If you're going to have a party, here's a fun snack you and your friends can make: Piccolo Pizza.

You'll Need:
- English Muffins (enough for all of you, plus seconds too!)
- One can of tomato sauce
- Oregano
- Grated cheese
- One package of hot dogs

1. Cut the muffins in half, and toast in a toaster or in the oven. If you're not allowed to use the oven by yourself, ask an adult for help.

2. Mix a small amount of oregano into the can of tomato sauce. Spread the sauce on each muffin half.

3. Slice the hot dogs into small pieces and place some on each muffin half.

4. Sprinkle grated cheese on top. Place the pizzas on a baking sheet and put them under the broiler for one to two minutes. Presto—neato piccolo pizzas!

TRICKY TREATS

Having a party? Here's a different and easy surprise you can make for yourself or members of your NEAT STUFF Club.

You'll need:
- A donut (more if you are serving friends)
- Plate and spoon
- Sherbet—any flavor you like
- Chocolate sauce
- Your favorite dry breakfast cereal

Place a donut on a plate. Add a scoop of sherbet over the donut hole. Pour on some chocolate sauce and sprinkle dry cereal on top.

Be sure to have enough for everyone!

FROZEN YOGURT SNACKOS

A snack that tastes great and is pretty healthy stuff, too.

You'll need:
- A container of your favorite fruit yogurt
- Two paper cups
- Two wooden sticks

Stir the yogurt till the fruit is well mixed. Pour into paper cups. Place wooden sticks in cup, and put in freezer. When the yogurt is frozen, peel off the cups and you've got a neat snacko!

JOKES AND RIDDLES

WHAT DID THE BIG TOE SAY TO THE LITTLE TOE?

DON'T LOOK NOW BUT A HEEL IS FOLLOWING US!

Tom: Did you hear the one about the sidewalk?
Toby: Yes, it's all over town.

Boy: Why is the letter "U" like a rabbit's foot?
Girl: Because it's always in luck!

Trout: Why are fisherman so stingy?
Glam: Because their business makes them shellfish.

Dad: What's green and dangerous?
Don: A thundering herd of pickles!

Pit: What kind of hobby does a shark like?
Pat: I can't even guess.
Pit: Anything it can sink its teeth into.

Betty: What goes up but never comes down?
Alice: Your age!

Silly: Help! I just heard a mouse squeak.
Sally: What do you want me to do, oil it?

Q: What do you call a frightened skin diver?
A: A chicken of the sea.

WHAT'S THE MOST IMPOSSIBLE THING IN THE WORLD TO DO?

PUTTING TOOTHPASTE BACK IN THE TUBE!

ARTS
AND CRAFTS

LIFE-SIZE POSTER OF YOURSELF

You can make a life-size poster of yourself and all the members of your NEAT STUFF Club. It's a great wall decoration. Also, it's a super gift for parents or grandparents. Here's how you do it.

Get large sheets of wrapping paper. The paper should be longer than your body. You can usually get wrapping paper from a butcher or florist shop. Art supply stores sell fancy colored paper which is also good for posters.

Work with a friend or club member. You lie down on the paper. Your friend draws all around your body. Trade off. On another piece of paper, you draw around your friend's body.

Then each of you can complete the poster with paint, crayons or colored markers. Draw clothes, hair and a face.

For fun, make a poster of each member of your NEAT STUFF Club. Try making posters of friends running, jumping or even dancing!

START A FINGERPRINT COLLECTION

No two people in the world have the same fingerprints. You can discover this if you start your own fingerprint collection. Fingerprint all the members of your NEAT STUFF Club, as well as members of your family.

All you need is some plain white paper and an ink pad. On the paper, draw ten squares (two sets of five squares), one for each finger. At the top of the paper, leave some room for a person's name.

Then, place the very tip of the person's finger on the ink pad. Be sure to see that the fingertip is evenly covered with ink.

Carefully and slowly roll the finger on one of the squares on the paper. If you press the finger down too hard, you'll smudge the print. Make sure you have a print of each finger in the ten squares.

Next, get a magnifying glass and look at the different designs in each fingerprint. Compare the prints of various people, and you'll notice many differences.

DISCOVERING FINGERPRINTS

Even though fingerprints left on objects are usually invisible, you can find them if you know how. To see fingerprints which are on a dark, smooth surface, you need baby or face powder and a small artist's paint brush.

Sprinkle the powder on the surface, such as a table top. Then, carefully dust off the extra powder with the paint brush. The remaining powder will stick to the fingerprints and make them visible.

Compare these fingerprints with the ones in your collection. See if you can match the newly discovered prints with those of family members or friends in your NEAT STUFF Club.

TRANSFERRING FINGERPRINTS

Sometimes fingerprints are very easy to see, especially if they have been left by a person with dirty hands. Most fingerprints cannot be seen on white or clear surfaces. But you can find these invisible fingerprints.

You'll need: Very dark chalk or charcoal dust, a small artist's brush, and cellophane tape.

Put a small bit of the dark powdered chalk or dust on a smooth surface where you suspect there might be fingerprints. Brush the area lightly until the fingerprints become visible. If none appear, then try again at another spot.

When you do find some fingerprints, you can transfer them by carefully covering the print with a piece of clear cellophane tape. Gently remove the tape. If done slowly, the powder will stick to the tape. Then attach the tape to a light-colored piece of paper. Compare the fingerprint with those in your collection.

AUTUMN LEAF COLLAGES

A collage (pronounced koh-laj) is a two-dimensional picture. You can make really unusual collages using different-colored autumn leaves.

As the leaves begin to fall, collect a lot of different-shaped ones in red, yellow or brown. Then, on a large piece of paper, draw or paint a tree trunk and branches. Glue the leaves to the branches.

When you're finished, you'll have a special, autumn-leaf collage.

BEECH

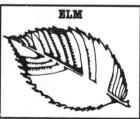

BIRCH

CHESTNUT

COTTONWOOD

ELM

HAWTHORN

MAPLE

HOW MANY OF THESE **LEAVES** ARE IN YOUR NEIGHBORHOOD?

OAK

PRESSING LEAVES

S tart a collection of leaves from the different trees in your neighborhood. Carry a thick book or newspaper with you, and carefully put each leaf between the pages. When you get home, press and dry the leaves.

Here's how: Place the leaves flat between two pieces of newspaper. Cover with heavy books for one week.

After the leaves are dry, you can use them for table decorations, placecards (write a person's name on the dry leaf with a marker), bulletin boards, or your scrapbook.

CRAFT CLAY CREATURES

You can make a whole collection of crazy creatures out of craft clay.

You'll need:
- 1 cup of corn starch
- 2 cups of baking soda
- 1 1/2 cups of water
- Food coloring
- Bread board
- Damp cloth

1. Put all the ingredients into a saucepan. Cook over medium heat on the stove. Stir constantly. If you are not allowed to use a stove, ask an adult to help you.

2. When the mixture begins to get stiff, pour it out on a bread board and knead it into a ball. Careful, it will be hot!

3. Then cover the clay with a damp cloth until it is cool.

4. When cool, take a small amount of clay and knead in the food coloring.

Make any type of animal, real or imaginary. Be sure to keep the unused clay covered with a damp cloth. Otherwise it will dry out quickly.

ORANGE POMANDERS

Many people enjoy hanging orange pomander balls in closets or putting them in drawers to make their clothes smell good.

You'll need:
- A big orange with fairly soft skin
- A box of cloves
- A pretty ribbon

Follow the instructions, and you'll have a pretty sweet gift.

1. With a pen or a pencil divide the orange into quarters across the top, as shown above.

2. Stick as many cloves as possible into each quarter, leaving the space between empty.

3. Tie a ribbon around the orange in the grooves between the cloves.

GO FLY A KITE!

Springtime is a windy time of year and a good time for kite flying. Dave Checkley of The Kite Factory in Seattle shares his original kite design with NEAT STUFF Club members. To make Dave's kite, you'll need:

- A plastic trash bag, 24 inches high or larger
- Two 2-foot-long by ⅛-inch-wide dowels
- Cellophane tape
- String
- A marker and scissors

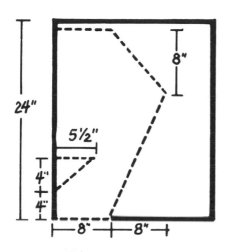

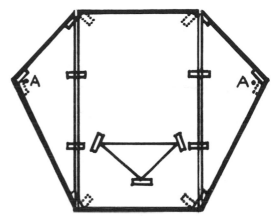

1. Spread the bag flat and mark the cutting pattern with a marker. Cut through both thicknesses of the bag, leaving the side edge intact. Unfold the bag.

2. Tape the dowels to the plastic, as shown. Wrap some tape over the ends of the dowels so they won't cut the plastic.

3. Cut triangular air vent, four inches up from the bottom of the bag, as shown. Reinforce the corners of the vent with tape.

4. Fold strips of tape over the wing tips as marked "A" in the diagram. Then punch holes in the tape for the bridle.

5. Cut a 10-foot length of string. Tie each end of the string to the holes. Tie a loop in the exact center of this string harness. Then tie a flying line to the loop.

To get your kite airborne, stand with your back to the wind. Hold onto the bridle loop and toss the kite into the air.

BUILDING CASTLES

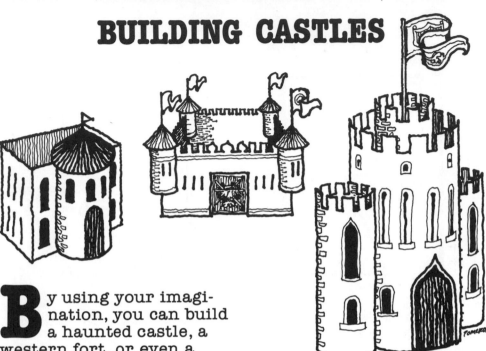

By using your imagination, you can build a haunted castle, a western fort, or even a whole town. It's easy and will be fun to play with for a long time.

You'll need:
- Six or more small cardboard boxes, tall tubes, round or different-sized packing containers
- Various colors of waterpaint and brushes
- Cellophane tape
- Colored construction paper
- Toothpicks

Glue or tape the boxes together to form a building. Place the tubes on end to form towers.

Paint your boxes the color of brick or in a design which looks like stone. When the paint dries, use a darker color and draw windows and doors. If you use wax milk cartons, cover them with construction paper, since paint will not stick to the

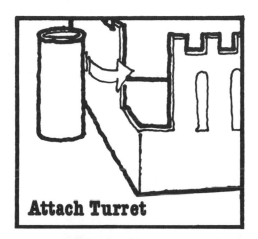

Attach Turret

Make Cone Roofs

Paint Flags

Drawbridge

waxed surface of milk cartons.

The toothpicks are the flag poles. Flags can be made out of colored paper.

Grass, bushes and flowers can also be made out of different colors of construction paper and glued to your buildings.

NIFTY NAPKINS FOR GIFTS

Napkins are a gift everyone can use. They can be any size or color, plain or decorated. Buy a package of paper napkins at the supermarket and follow these directions.

If you want, you can also use a potato stamp to make gift-wrapping paper. Get white paper at a florist, butcher shop or art supply store. Cut to whatever size you want, then stamp the potato design all over the paper.

1. CUT A BIG POTATO IN HALF. DRAW YOUR DESIGN ON BACKWARDS WITH A PEN OR MARKER.

2. WITH A KNIFE, CAREFULLY CUT OUT THE DESIGN UNTIL IT'S ABOUT A HALF INCH THICK.

3. WHEN THE DESIGN IS CUT OUT, POUR SOME PAINT OR VEGETABLE DYE INTO A FLAT DISH, DIP THE POTATO IN THE PAINT, THEN STAMP IT FIRMLY ON THE NAPKIN. GIVE YOURSELF A FEW EXTRA NAPKINS FOR PRACTICING.

ANIMATED STORY BOOK

You can make your own animated story book. The characters, people, or animals will actually look as though they move. You'll need a pad of paper, with a dozen or more pages, and a pencil.

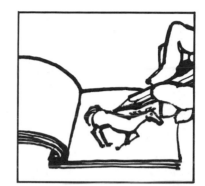

1. Draw a simple figure on a back page of the pad of paper.

2. On the same spot of each page going towards the front, draw the figure in a different position.

3. Quickly flip the pages and your figure will move.

Draw a person or animal. Moving the position of the legs will make it appear as though a person is dancing. An animal can wink by changing the position of the eye from wide-open to half-open to closed.

After animating one character, try a whole story with lots of different people and animals!

JOKES AND RIDDLES

Q: What do you do when an elephant sneezes?
A: Get out of the way.

Mit: What do you call a lieutenant's boss in the corn army?
Mat: A kernel.

She: What building has the most stories?
He: The library.

Ferd: What do you get when you cross a bat with a mummy?
Nann: Either a flying bandage or a gift-wrapped bat.

Will: Why do humming birds hum?
f9Because they don't know the words.

Diner: Do you have soup on the menu?
Waiter: We did, but I just wiped it off.

Kathy: What are the four seasons?
Linda: Salt, pepper, mustard and ketchup!

Knock Knock
Who's there?
Thistle!
Thistle who?
Thistle be the last knock knock joke on this page.

Sue: Why did the pink panther bring a rope to the baseball game?
Sal: So he could tie the score.

Neat Stuff

PETS

SELECTING A KITTEN

Pets are fun to own and a pleasure to feed and love. If you are thinking about getting a kitten, here are some points to consider before saying, "I want that one!"

Usually the best time to get a kitten is when it is six to eight weeks old. Then it will be house-broken, weaned from its mother, and old enough to be your pet.

1. *Eyes should be clear and free of irritation and tears.*

2. *Fur should be glossy without any bare spots.*

3. *Body should be firm and free of rashes.*

4. *Ears should be clean and alert.*

5. *Gums should be pink and free of sores.*

6. *Skin should not have lumps or any redness.*

SELECTING A PUPPY

Selecting the right puppy for you is very important since the animal will be a member of your family for ten or more years. Before you start looking at real, furry, cuddly puppies, think about these points:

- Are the puppy's parents' big? It usually means that the puppy will grow into a big dog. Do you want a dog that size?
- Do you have a big enough yard in which a large dog can exercise?
- If you live in an apartment, will there be enough room for the dog?
- Will a shedding, long-hair dog upset any member of your family? Some people are allergic to dog hair.

Once you've decided on the type of puppy you want, here are some serious things to consider:

- Is the puppy old enough to leave its mother? Usually, the puppy should be at least six to eight weeks old before it leaves its mother. The older the puppy, the easier it will be to house train.
- Is the puppy healthy? Its nose should be cold, its eyes clear, and there should be no sores on its body.
- How does the puppy act? Avoid shy dogs or puppies that snap. Either could be trouble.

PETS TO AVOID

Once in a while, every-one dreams of owning a strange or different type of pet. Some people are just not satisfied with a dog, a cat, some fish or even a hamster. But it may be against the law to keep unusual animals.

Strange or "exotic" pets can cause their owners a great many problems. For example:

- Unusual pets are very difficult to feed. The right kind of food for them may be hard to find and expensive to buy.
- Exotic pets are usually native to warm or very hot climates. This means you'll have a problem keeping them warm and happy.
- Strange pets are difficult to cage. It is usually necessary to keep them in special cages for their protection as well as yours.

Here are some of the pets you'll want to avoid: snakes (even the harmless garden variety), monkeys, alligators, large tropical birds (unless you really know what you're doing), wolves, foxes, and even chicks and ducks (unless you live on a farm or have very understanding neighbors).

Play it smart. Let the zoo keep the unusual animals.

JOKES AND RIDDLES

AND NOW THE BIG DILL OF THE DAY!!

Bee: What's every pickle's favorite TV game show?
Bop: "Let's Make a Dill."

Judge: Have you ever been up before me?
Prisoner: I don't know what time you get up!

Lee: What goes HA HA HA Plop?
Jim: I don't know.
Lee: Someone who laughs his or her head off.

Chuck: What's red, white, blue and yellow?
Evelyn: I don't know. What?
Chuck: A star-spangled banana.

Jack: What do you put in a box to make it weigh less?
Jean: I don't know; tell me
Jack: A hole!

Jenny: Where do moths dance?
Denny: I don't know.
Jenny: They dance at moth balls.

Milly: I spent the summer in Switzerland
Tilly: Berne?
Milly: No, I nearly froze.

Teacher: Do you keep stationery at your desk?
Bob: For a while, then I just have to move a little!

Prisoner just out of jail: At last, I'm free. I'm free.
Young Child: So what, I'm four.

Pit: What has four legs but can't walk?
Bit: What?
Pit: A chair.

JOKES AND RIDDLES

BURRRP!!!

Jill: Last night I dreamed that I ate a five-pound marshmallow.
Joe: So what?
Jill: When I woke up this morning my pillow was gone!

Tam: What happens when you cross a potato with a sponge?
Pam: You get a terrible-tasting thing that soaks up lots of gravy.

Barbara: I don't like the look of that halibut.
Waiter: If you want good looks, then order goldfish!

WHY DID THE CROW SIT ON THE TELEPHONE WIRE?

HE WANTED TO MAKE A LONG-DISTANCE CAW!

Bo: There's lots of juice in this grapefruit.
Peep: I'll say, more than meets the eye.

Ray: What is a greasy flyer?
Better: I don't know.
Ray: A dirty bird.

Fred: What is long and purple, and has eleven legs and eyes that glow in the dark?
Ned: I don't know.
Fred: I don't either, but it sure looks strange there on your arm!

Knock Knock
Who's there?
Olive
Olive who?
Olive you.

Joe: What is the difference between a thief and a church?
Moe: One steals from the people and the other peals from the steeple.